Cric

Amazing Ideas To Create With Your Cricut Machine

Written By

Kayla Machine

Table of Contents

INTRODUCTION

Thank you for purchasing this book!

Cricut has for some time been a popular brand under crafted by Provo Craft. Many individuals have long overlooked the craft of scrapbooking and paper patterns, as people dive into the new universe of advanced workmanship and makeovers. Luckily, there are still organizations like Cricut, who has high respect with regards to the customary types of expressions and artworks. For over forty years, Provo Craft had the option to give probably the most dazzling centerpieces roused by the most splendid wellsprings of imagination. Being a universal producer, the creators of Cricut have gradually extended to various pieces of the globe, giving boundless chances to numerous craftsmen and vendors. With its responsibility to give simply the best in the field of expressions and artworks, Cricut had the option to dispatch the absolute most surprising materials that are viewed as the must-have accumulation for each craftsman.

One of the most prevalent of the Cricut items is the Cricut shaper machine. By introducing a cartridge into the shaper, different shapes and plans can be made by any devoted specialties laborer. A ton of people set aside a ton of cash for this gadget, given its extraordinary guide with regards to planning. There are additionally the individuals who like to utilize the Cricut Expression line that digs in progressively expound designs, including silk screens and the utilization of vinyl and card stock. All machines are additionally utilizing the cartridges made by Cricut to concoct different themes and layouts.

Enjoy your reading!

Cricut Design Space

How do I Get Started?

The Cricut Design Space application is one that is run entirely from your web browser. This means that you will need an active internet connection in order to use it but downloading that plugin will allow you to jump in and out of the Cricut Design Space as you please from your device. This plugin will allow you to log in from your computer and your login information will allow you to download the plugin on any device you choose, so you can move from computer to computer with ease!

Upon your first login to the Cricut Design Space, you will be prompted to inform the program of the type of Cricut machine that you'd like to install. This will tell the program what type of machine it will be communicating with so it can ensure that it is properly laying out all your cuts, lines, and scores. Once you've completed this step and your computer has properly identified your device, you will want to click the "New Project" button that's situated in the upper right-hand corner. This is where you will be prompted to download the installer for the Cricut Design Space plugin that will allow your computer and Cricut Design Space to connect with one another.

Opening the Cricut Design Space Plugin Installer for the first time will prompt you to link your device to the Cricut machine that you've selected. Establishing this connection will allow your computer to communicate seamlessly with your Cricut machine. Once the connection is established between your computer and your machine, you will be able to create projects whenever you'd like without having to reestablish that connection. This means that you can import images from other sources, images that you've created by yourself, or you can use any of the numerous images that Cricut offers either for free through Cricut Design Space or through their paid Access subscription.

The first thing you should know about Cricut Access is that *it is not required that you have this subscription to use Cricut Design Space*. You can make use of Cricut Design Space and every feature that it has to offer without worrying about being stuck behind a paywall.

The benefits that a crafter gets from signing up for a Cricut Access membership will vary depending on the subscription tier that you have chosen. At this time, there are three subscription tiers available through the Cricut Access program.

Monthly - $9.99 per month

With this monthly tier of the Cricut Access Subscription, you will receive unlimited use of over 400 fonts that are available to use right within Cricut Design Space, the unlimited and unrestricted usage of over 90,000 images that you can use for any design you wish in the Cricut Design Space, 10% member savings on your purchases made from the Cricut website, including items that are already on sale, as well as a 10% savings on licensed fonts and ready-to-make projects from supported brands like Sanrio, Disney, Simplicity, and Anna Griffin.

Annual - $7.99 per month, billed once per annum at $95.88

With this annual tier of the Cricut Access Subscription, you will receive unlimited use of over 400 fonts that are available to use right within Cricut Design Space, the unlimited and unrestricted usage of over 90,000 images that you can use for any design you wish in the Cricut Design Space, 10% member savings on your purchases made from the Cricut website, including items that are already on sale, as well as a 10% savings on licensed fonts and ready-to-make projects from supported brands like Sanrio, Disney, Simplicity, and Anna Griffin. In addition to these features, which are also available through the Cricut Access monthly subscription, you will gain access to a Priority Member Care Line, which cuts your wait time for customer support calls in half.

Premium - $9.99 per month, billed once per annum at $119.88

With this premium tier of the Cricut Access Subscription, you will receive unlimited use of over 400 fonts that are available to use right within Cricut Design Space, the unlimited and unrestricted usage of over 90,000 images that you can use for any design you wish in the Cricut Design Space, 10% member savings on your purchases made from the Cricut website, including items that are already on sale, as well as a 10% savings on licensed fonts and ready-to-make projects from supported brands like Sanrio, Disney, Simplicity, and Anna Griffin. In addition to these features, which are also available through the Cricut Access monthly subscription, you will gain access to a Priority Member Care Line, which cuts your wait time for customer support calls in half. These features are added to your subscription with the annual membership. When you upgrade to the premium membership, you will also receive up to 50% savings on licensed fonts, images, and ready-to-make projects, and free economy shipping from the official Cricut website on all orders over $50.

These member perks can make all the difference for the crafter that is avidly creating lots of projects in a short period of time. Again, these subscriptions are in no way compulsory for crafters who wish to make use of the Cricut Design Space or its user-friendly interface, but these substantial benefits are what you can expect from the membership, should you choose to sign up!

Your First Design

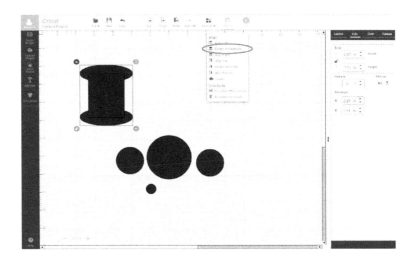

The first thing that will be presented to you when you launch Cricut Design Space for the first time is a quick tutorial on how to insert a shape into the Cricut Design Space, as well as how to fill that inserted shape with a colored pattern. You will want to give that process a few trial runs until you're perfectly familiar with all the steps and various assets and options. You will want to be able to introduce a shape into Cricut Design Space, change its Linetype, and change what the space is filled with. Once you've mastered that, you will have quite the head start on figuring out how to do more projects within the Cricut Design Space.

https://learn.cricut.com/design-space-for-beginners is a wonderful resource with a vast number of tutorial videos for various projects you can make, troubleshooting you can do with your Cricut machine, and so much more that will be useful to the Cricut crafter on the rise!

Now that you've gotten a bit of an introduction to the basics of Cricut Design Space, let's run through a quick project to get you familiar with the entire process.

In the first step, you will need to select the "Text" option. In the text box that appears, you're going to type the phrase "Good Vibes," and pick a font that's available in the Cricut Design Space that you like for this project. Do keep in mind that some of the fonts that are available in Cricut Design Space do come with a cost. If you're looking to find only fonts that are free, you can simply choose the "System Fonts," which limits you only to the fonts that are already installed on your computer. The positive here is that you can find fonts from other sources and use them to suit your specific needs!

Once you've chosen a font that is right for you and your project, make sure that the "Linetype" is set to "cut." Once you've checked this and made sure that the settings are appropriate, you can click "Make it," in the upper right-hand corner of your screen and follow the prompts that come up on the screen. If the design looks like it's properly placed on the screen that pops up following this step, then you'll continue on to the next steps.

You will notice that, at the top of the screen, there are helpful little measurements. Using those measurements, you can cut a piece of self-adhesive vinyl that is sized appropriately to accommodate the design you've created. Using your light blue or light grip Cricut Maker mat, you can line up your vinyl, so it lines up with the design on your screen. Your design will be cut directly from the piece you're layering onto the mat. If you need to make adjustments to your design, now is the perfect time to do so!

Once your vinyl is right where you need it to be and your design has been adjusted to your specification, you can use the scraper/burnishing tool to smooth your vinyl down onto the gripped surface of your mat. Using the back of the tool will help it to glide more smoothly without leaving any scratches on your vinyl. You will want to smooth it down from the middle, working outward toward the edges. Make sure that your piece is lying completely flat and that no folds, bubbles, or imperfections form along the way. This will give you the sharpest, cleanest, crispest cuts possible.

Now that your vinyl has been properly burnished onto the mat and you're ready to move on, you will want to set your Cricut machine to the "vinyl" setting so your machine applies the blade to the material with the appropriate pressure for your material. You may skip this step if you have a Cricut Maker, as that model will do this part automatically. Slide your mat under the mat guides in your Cricut machine. Once you've done that, you can click "Continue" on the bottom right of Cricut Design Space and the site will begin to communicate with your machine. Once it's in the right place, push the mat toward the rollers and click the flashing Load/Unload button that is marked with a double arrow. This will load the mat into the machine and lock it into place do your cuts are more precise.

Once the Cricut C button begins to flash, you should press it once and watch your Cricut machine go to work. Once the machine has completed its cut, remove the mat from the machine and bring it into your crafting space. Using the rounded back of your scraper/burnishing tool, you'll need to smooth down the entire surface of the vinyl on your mat. This will help the design to release more independently from the mat while you're weeding.

Once the vinyl has been thoroughly burnished, you will use the weeding tool to pick up the blanks in the centers of and surrounding the letters in your design. Once you've done this, you will find that all that's left on the carrier sheet is your design. This is when you will layer your transfer tape onto your design and burnish it completely. Once it's fully burnished with your scraper/burnishing tool, you will want to use rubbing alcohol to cleanse the surface that you wish to emblazon your design. I chose the back of my laptop.

Line up the transfer tape and your design up with the surface onto which you intend to put your design. Lay the design down and, using the scraper/burnishing tool, work out all the bubbles and imperfections until the design is clinging completely flat and snug to the surface that you've chosen. Now, using the thin side of your scraper/burnishing tool, pull up one corner of the transfer tape and slowly roll the tape back until it has lifted completely off of the surface and your design, taking take to press the letters down in any places where they might try to come up along the way.

Once your transfer tape has come away from your surface, you should be left to admire your very first Cricut project! Great work!

How Cricut Software Works

Design Space is a cloud-based software, which means all the information included in Design Space – including your projects and designs – is stored on remote servers hosted on the internet, rather than on your own personal computer. With the Design Space cloud, you can access your projects anywhere and from any device, not just your personal computer.

The most recent version of Design Space is Design Space 3. You can use Design Space 3 using either a Windows or a Mac operating system; you'll need Windows 8 or later or macOS 10.13 or later. To use Design Space from a device like a tablet or smartphone, you'll need iOS 11 or later or Android 6.0 or higher. Generally speaking, you will also need a good internet connection to access Design Space, particularly if you plan to connect to your Cricut through Bluetooth; however, if you have enough memory on your laptop or your iOS device (iPhone or iPad) and just want to begin designing a project rather than actually cutting it, you can also run Design Space offline. You cannot run Design Space using a Chromebook or Linux computer, as those work on different operating systems.

What Can You Do Using Design Space?

Settings

In Design Space, you will see a main drop-down menu on the top left-hand side of your screen, denoted by three horizontal lines. From this menu, you can navigate back to the homepage (Home) or go to your canvas (Canvas). You will also see many other setting options under this menu to help you set up your machine. You can create settings for custom materials, link physical Cricut cartridges to your account, calibrate your machine for specific blades, view your Cricut Access subscription, manage your overall Cricut account, and update your Design Space firmware to get the latest features.

Starting a New Project

When you're ready to start a new Cricut project, you'll begin by logging into Design Space using the username and password you registered with Cricut. Once you're logged in, you'll see the Design Space homepage. This page includes video tutorials, featured Cricut Access projects, and projects using new materials and tools. It also features a slider showcasing your most recently opened projects, making it easy to review what you've been working on and pick up where you left off.

At the top right-hand side of your screen, you have two options: a green New Project button and a My Projects button. To continue editing a project you've already started, click My Projects (you can also select a specific project using the aforementioned slider further down on the homepage). To start a brand new project, click the green New Project button. This will open a blank canvas, which is a screen with gridlines to help you properly measure and scale your project as you create. At the top of the canvas is your toolbar, which you will use to edit your design.

Creating and Editing Your Project

Once you begin a new project, on the left-hand side of your canvas, you will see a menu with several options: New, Templates, Projects, Images, Text, Shapes, and Upload. The New tab allows you to begin a new project;

when you click this option, you'll be prompted to save whatever you're working on.

The Templates tab brings up a wide range of templates, such as mugs or tea towels, that you can insert onto your blank canvas. These templates can help you better visualize what your design will look like and how to properly size and space images and text. The templates are for reference only and will not actually be cut as part of your design.

The Projects tab houses Cricut's Ready to Make projects. With these designs, you can just open a project and begin cutting – no need for any editing on your part. You can search these projects by category using the drop-down menu. Categories include specific types of project, such as accessories and home decor, as well as collections of free projects. Some of these ready-made designs do allow you to customize features, such as changing the text to personalize your project. Once you are ready to cut your selected project, simply click the Make It button on the lower right-hand corner of your screen; this will bring up a new mat preview screen where you can select the size of material you want to use and the number of copies you want to make. Design Space will even tell you which type of machine mat to use for the project.

The Images tab brings up the Cricut Image Library, which contains hundreds of graphics you can purchase to use in your design. You can search these images by category or if you are looking for a very specific type of image, you can type it into the search bar. If you see a small green "a" in the top left-hand corner of an image, that means that image is included in your Cricut Access. There is also a Free This Week category.

You can also use the Cartridges button to look through the image sets contained on various cartridges; these sets are then available for you to purchase to add to your personal Design Space library.

The Text tab opens up a text box on your canvas. You can type in your personalized text and then use the toolbar above the canvas to customize your font type, style, size, spacing, and alignment. You can also use this toolbar to curve your lettering and create shadowing effects. The Font drop-down box on the left-hand side of your toolbar allows you to select fonts included on your computer, as well as special Cricut fonts that are either included in your Cricut Access subscription or available for purchase. The Filter option in this menu allows you to search for fonts of a specific style, such as writing fonts or multi-layer fonts. To create a handwritten look, select a font that is a "writing" style; when you cut a project using this font, your Cricut will use pens to write your text as if it were done by hand. Cursive fonts fall under the writing style category. Fonts that are not writing styles, on the other hand, will appear on your final project as just the outline of the text, meaning the letters will not be filled in.

The Shapes tab brings up basic shapes, like circles or stars, that you can use in your design. You can edit these shapes, including their size and color, using the toolbar at the top of the canvas.

The Upload tab lets you select image files from your computer or device to use in your design. You can upload a range of file types, including .jpg, .gif, .png, .bmp, .svg, or .dxf. You can also upload an image or pattern to use as a fill, or background, for your project.

On the right-hand side of your canvas, you will see another menu with a tab for Layers and a tab for Color Sync. If your canvas is blank, this menu will be grayed out, meaning you will not be able to click on any of the options. However, once you have inserted an image, graphic, text box, or shape onto your blank canvas, you will be able to click through this menu as well. Each item on your canvas – each image, text box, graphic, or shape – sits in its own layer and is editable independently of all the other design items. The Layer menu includes options in the lower right-hand corner to customize each layer. The Slice option allows you to split overlapping layers into separate pieces, while the Weld option lets you merge two or more layers. Use the Attach option to hold a layer in place to make your cut or to add a text box to a shape or image layer; if you do not use this button, the Cricut machine may move the design on that layer when it cuts in order to maximize the use of your material. The Flatten option merges all of your layers into a "flat" printable image, while the Contour option lets you see or hide lines on a particular layer.

When you click on a particular layer, you will see a pop-up menu called Layer Attributes. This is where you can assign a color to your layer (for example, making a star shape yellow) and select whether that particular layer will be cut, written, or scored by your Cricut machine.

The Layer menu also includes a Color Sync option, which helps you match colors between layers. This is useful when you are using multiple colors in a single project; the Color Sync feature ensures that your Cricut machine cuts all layers that are the same color at the same time, removing the need for you to switch materials back and forth multiple times.

Cutting Your Project

When you are happy with your design, click the green Make It button in the top right-hand side of your screen. This will bring up your mat preview screen (mentioned previously). In this screen, you can select the number of copies you want to cut and the size of the design. You can also rotate your designs and move them so that they sit exactly where you want on your mat. For example, if your project includes five small star shapes, you can arrange them in a single line at the top of your mat rather than scattered around the mat; in this way, you can maximize the space on your material and cut down on material waste.

When your designs are arranged to your liking, make sure that your Cricut machine is connected to your computer or device, either through the USB cable or wirelessly via Bluetooth. Click the green Continue button in the lower right-hand side of your screen, and your machine will begin your cut.

Practice, Practice, Practice

If you owned a legacy Cricut model that functioned using physical cartridges, the Design Space software may seem a bit intimidating at first. However, the freedom the software gives you in terms of creating unique, truly customized projects is well worth the effort it takes to learn the program. The best way to become more comfortable with the software is simply to spend some time clicking through and exploring all of its capabilities and experimenting with new designs. As with anything else, practice makes perfect!

Simple Operation with Cricut

Imputing

If you're new to Cricut or have little experience using one, it can be quite intimidating. I've had friends tell me they can't figure out how to use theirs, or they feel they aren't getting the full benefits of the machine. Cricut can be daunting, especially for the newbie or inexperienced.

I'm sure you're anxious to start your first project, and understandably so. You've seen all the amazing things it can do and ideas are swirling in your mind. Cards, gifts, home decorations… you can't wait!

But wait! You want to prevent disasters and, yes, they can happen, so let's start from the beginning.

The Cricut Design Space is cutting software that has a canvas area where you'll do your design work, such as uploading images. It also provides a plethora of fonts.

Before you do anything, you'll need to go to the Cricut website and set up an account. This will provide you with a homepage that will be unique to you. Sign-up is simple and free. You'll need to create an access ID and password.

Once you've set up your account, you'll want to go to your page, which is broken down into six areas: canvas, design panel, edit and text edit bar, layer panel and color sync panel.

The design panel allows you to start a new project, complete a project, add images and upload your own images. There is also an edit bar so you can undo an action and redo it if necessary.

The tool bar at the top gives you plenty of options to layout your work by aligning it, size, rotate, etc. You'll find almost all the same tools as you would in a Microsoft Word toolbar.

Loading and unloading paper

If you're particularly into paper craft, you will find the edge distresser, quilling tool, piercing tool, and craft mat in this set to be essential in your crafting. Quilling or paper filigree art is more popular than ever these days and these are some of the best tools available for that craft.

One hack that a number of craters, bloggers, and YouTubers swear by is buying contact paper from either Target or the Dollar Tree and using it at transfer tape! Contact paper is available nearly everywhere and you can get a lot of it for a very reasonable price. The adhesive on contact paper is meant to be removed after months or even years of use with little to no residue. This quality makes it a great substitute for transfer tape, which we rely on to keep all our project pieces exactly in place between the carrier sheet and our project materials!

When loading paper onto a cricut machine, follow the following steps:

1. Fold your 12x 12 paper into half. There are some designs that are already precut for you.

2. Remove the cover on your mat

3. Line the paper on the mat and make sure it sticks

4. Hold the mat firmly against the rollers and press the button "Load Paper"

Selecting shapes letters and phrases

In order for the cricut machine to cut, you must select the phrases, letters and/or shapes that it will cut. The phrases, letters and shapes that you select appear on the display screen of the Cricut machine.

Remove your cut from cutting mat

One of the things to do in setting up and using your machine is to do a test cut every time you start a project, especially with a new material. Do not be lazy on this—testing out your cut only takes a few seconds, and it goes a long way. Doing a test cut means you do not need to do other time-costing cuts. You'll also know if the pressure you're putting on is enough to cut the material but not the mat.

To remove the cut from the mat all you need to do is make use of the tool set. The tool set consists of various tools that are meant to help you remove the cut from the cutting mat with ease.

Complex Operations

Cricut machines are pretty straightforward with what you need to do in order to make simple designs, but you might wonder about some of the more complex operations. Here, we'll tell you how to accomplish these with just a few simple button presses.

<u>Blade Navigation and Calibration</u>

The blades that come with a Cricut machine are important to understand, and you will need to calibrate your blades every single time you use your machine.

Each blade needs this because it will help you figure out which level of depth and pressure your cut needs to be. Typically, each blade needs to be calibrated only once, which is great, because then you don't have to spend time doing this each time. Once you've done it once, it will stay calibrated, but if you decide to change the housings of the blades or if you use them in another machine, you'll need to calibrate it again.

So, if you plan on using a knife blade and then a rotary blade, you'll want to make sure that you do recalibrate – and make sure you do this before you start with your project. It is actually incredibly easy to do this though, which is why it's encouraged.

To calibrate a blade, you just launch the Design Space, and from there, you open the menu and choose calibration. Then, choose the blade that you're going to put in. For the purpose of this explanation, let's say you're using a knife blade.

Put that blade in the clamp B area and do a test cut, such as with copy paper into the mat, and then load that into the machine.

Press continue, then press the go button on the machine. It will then do everything that you need for the item itself, and it will start to cut.

You can then choose which calibration is best for your blade, but usually, the first one is good enough.

You can do this with every blade you use, and every time you use a new blade on your machine, I highly recommend you do this – for best results, of course.

Set Paper Size

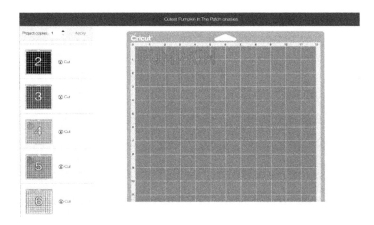

Setting paper size in a Cricut machine is actually pretty simple. You will want to use this with either cartridge or with Design Space for what you'd like to make. This also comes with a cutting mat, and you'll want to load this up with paper so that you can use it.

To do this, you'll want to make sure that you have it plugged in, then go to the project preview screen. If you choose a material that's bigger than the mat size, it will automatically be changed, and it'll be adjusted as necessary based on the size of the material that you select.

You can choose the color, the size of the material, whether or not it'll mirror – and you can also choose to fully skip the mat, too, if you don't want that image printed just yet.

Note that the material size menu does offer sizes that are bigger than the largest mat available.

If you're planning on using the print then cut mode, do understand that it's limited to a print area of 8.5x11 inches, but again, you can choose these settings for yourself.

Load Last

To load that paper and image last is pretty simple. Remember the preview we discussed in the previous section? Remember that "skip this mat" step? Literally, press that, and then go. You'll be able to skip this quite easily. It's one of those operations that's definitely a little different from what you may be used to, but if you want to skip design and don't want to work with it just yet, this is probably the best option for you to use. If you're worried about forgetting it, don't worry – Cricut will remind you.

Paper Saver

Saving paper is something you'll want to consider doing with a Cricut machine because it loves to eat up the paper before you even start decorating. The Explore Air 2 definitely will appreciate it if you save paper, and there are a few ways to do so.

The first one is, of course, to halve your mats. But you don't need to do only that.

You can also go to the material saver option on the machine, which will automatically adjust and align your paper as best it can. Unfortunately, on newer machines, it's actually not directly stated, but there is a way to save paper on these.

You'll want to create tabbed dividers to organize your projects and save them directly there.

The first step is to create a background shape. Make sure that the paper looks like a background. Go to shapes, and then select the square to make the square shape.

Next, once you've created squares to represent the paper, arrange this to move to the back so that the shapes are organized to save the most space on each mat. Then organize the items that are on top of where the background is and arrange them so they all fit on a singular mat.

Rotating is your best friend – you can use this feature whenever you choose objects, so I do suggest getting familiarized with it.

Next, you hide the background at this point, and you do this by choosing the square, and in Design Space, literally hiding this on the right side. Look at the eyeball on the screen, and you'll see a line through the eyeball. That means it's hidden.

Check over everything and fine-tune it at this point. Make sure they're grouped around one object, and make sure everything has measurements. Move these around if they're outside of the measurements required.

Once they're confirmed, you then attach these together on the right-hand side of Design Space, which keeps everything neatly together – they're all cut from the same sheet.

From here, repeat this until everything is neatly attached. It will save your paper, but will it save you time? That's debatable, of course.

Speed Dial

So, the speed dial typically comes into play when you're setting the pressure and speed. Fast mode is one of the options available on the Explore Air 2 and the Maker machines, which make the machine run considerably faster than other models. You can use this with vinyl, cardstock, and iron-on materials. To set this, go to the cut screen. You'll have a lot of speed dials here, and various different settings. If you have the right material in place when choosing it, you'll be given the option to do it quickly with fast mode. From there, you simply tap or click on that switch in order to toggle this to the position for on. That will activate fast mode for that item.

It will make everything about two times faster, which means that if you're making complex swirl designs, it will take 30 seconds instead of the 73-second average it usually takes.

However, one downside to this is that because it's so fast, it will sometimes make the cuts less precise – you'll want to move back to the regular mode for finer work.

This is all usually set with the smart-set dial, which will offer the right settings for you to get the best cuts that you can on any material you're using. Essentially, this dial eliminates you having to manually check the pressure on this.

To change the speed and pressure for a particular material that isn't already determined with the preset settings, you will need to select custom mode and choose what you want to create. Of course, the smart-set dial is better for the Cricut products and mats. If you notice that the blade is cutting too deep or not deep enough, there is a half-settings option on each material that you can adjust to achieve the ideal cut.

Usually, the way you do this with the pre-set settings is to upload and create a project, press go, and load the mat, then move the smart-set dial on the machine itself to any setting. Let's select custom and choose the speed for this one.

In Design Space, you then choose the material, add the custom speed, and you can adjust these settings. You can even adjust the number of times you want the cut to be changed with the smart-set dial, too. Speed is something you can adjust to suit the material, which can be helpful if you're struggling with putting together some good settings for your items.

Pressure Dial

Now, let's talk about pressure. Each piece of material will require different pressure settings. If you're not using enough pressure, the blade won't cut into the material, and if you use too much pressure, you'll end up cutting the mat, which isn't what you want to do.

The smart-set dial kind of takes the guesswork out of it. You simply choose the setting that best fits your material, and from there, you let it cut. If you notice you're not getting a deep enough cut, then you'll want to adjust it about half a setting to get a better result. From there, adjust as needed.

But did you know that you can change the pressure on the smart-set dial for custom materials? Let's say you're cutting something that's very different, such as foil, and you want to set the pressure to be incredibly light so that the foil doesn't get shredded. What you do is you load the material in, and you choose the custom setting. You can then choose the material you plan to cut, such as foil – and if it's not on the list, you can add it.

From here, you're given pressure options. Often, people will go too heavy with their custom settings, so I do suggest that you go lighter for the first time and change it as needed. There is a number of draggers that goes from low to high. If you need lots of pressure, obviously let it go higher. If you don't need much pressure, make sure it's left lower. You will also want to adjust the number of times the cut is done on a multi-cut feature item.

This is a way for you to achieve multiple cuts for the item, which can be incredibly helpful for those who are trying to get the right cut, or if the material is incredibly hard to cut. I don't suggest using this for very flimsy and thin material, because it'll just waste your blade and the mat itself.

That's all there is to it! This is a great way to improve on your Cricut designs. Personally, I love to work with custom cuts, and you can always delete these if you feel like they don't work. You just press the change settings button to adjust your pressure, speed, or how many cuts you want, and then choose to save when you're done.

What if you don't like a setting, period? You can delete it, of course!

To delete, go to materials settings, and you'll see a little trash can next to it. Press the trash can, and the setting will be removed.

Adjusting the pressure and cuts is part of why people love using Design Space, and it's a great feature to try.

Cricut Design Space

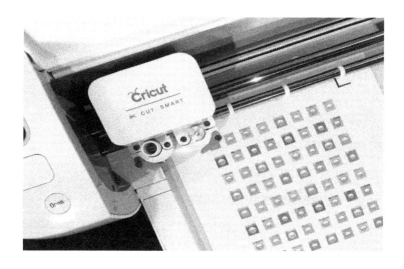

Design Space lets you do many things with your Cricut machine. Here are a few things you can do with this convenient app:

- Aligning various items right next to one another.

- Attaching items to hold images in place, and lets you use score lines.

- Arranging these to make them sit on the canvas in different layers.

- Canvas, a tool that lets you arrange prints and vectors so you can use the various tools with them.

- Contouring, which is a tool that lets you hide image layers quickly, so they're not cut out.

- Color sync, which lets you use multiple colors in one project to reduce the material differences.

- Cut buttons, which will start cuts.

- Make it button: this is the screen that lets you see the designs being cut.

- Draw lines: lets you draw with the pen to write images and such.

- Fill: lets you fill in a pattern or color on an item.

- Flipping items flip it horizontally or vertically by 180 degrees.

- Group: puts different text and images on a singular layer, and everything is moved at once so that it doesn't affect the layout.

- Linetype: an option that you can do with your piece, whether you want to cut a line, draw a line, or score a line.

- Mirrored image: reverses it, which is very important with transfer vinyl, so everything reads correctly.

- Print then Cut: it's an option that lets you print the design, and from there, the machine cuts it.

- Redo: does an action again and reverses it.

- Reverse Weeding: removes the vinyl that's left behind, and it's used mostly for stencil vinyl

- Score lines: helps you make creases in the papers so you can fold it.

- SVG: this is a scalable vector graphic that lets you cut a file that's scaled to be larger or smaller so that the resolution is kept, and made up of lines that consist of infinite white dots.

- Texts and fonts: let you use put specialized fonts and words within Design Space.

- Weeding: lets you remove the excess vinyl from designs. Press this when you're cutting vinyl.

- Welding: a tool you use when you want to combine two line shapes into one shape, and it's used to make seamless cursive words.

These are most of the functions you can do in Design Space. To use these, simply choose an image or font that you want to use and put it in Design Space. From there, you can do literally whatever you need to do with it – within reason, of course – and then put the image onto the material that you're using. For the purposes of learning, I suggest not getting in too deep with vinyl just yet, and get used to using these tools. You also have pens, which can be implemented to help you write images with a tool that looks sharp and crisp. We'll go over the purpose of pens and what you can do with them in the next section.

Cricut Pens

Pens for your Cricut machine are essentially another way to get creative with your projects. I love to use them for cards, handmade tags for gifts, or even fancy invites and labels.

Now, each pen offers a little different finish and point size. They aren't toxic, and they are permanent once they're dried. You've got the extra-fine points for small lettering, up to a medium tip for making thicker lines. There are also glitter and metallic pens, so you have a lot of options to choose from!

But do you have to use them? Well, the answer is no. You can use different pens, but test them on paper first and get adapters to use with them. Cricut pens are your best option.

To use these, choose the wording or design, or whatever you want to do. You want to go to the layers panel that's on the right-hand side, and choose the scissors icon – change that to the write icon. From there, you'll want to choose the pen color that you would like to use.

You can then have the design printed out on the material you're using.

Some people like to use different fonts, whether it be system fonts or Cricut fonts, or the Cricut Access fonts. However, the one thing with Design Space is that it will write what will normally be cut, so you'll get an outline of that font rather than just a solid stroke of writing.

This can add to the design, however – you essentially change the machine from cut to write, and there you go.

You can also use the Cricut writing fonts, which you can choose by going to a blank canvas, and then choosing the text tool on the left-hand side, along with the wording you'd like for this to have.

Once you're in the font edit toolbar, you are given a font selection. You choose the writing font filter, so you have fonts that you can write with. From there, choose the font, and then switch from the scissors to the pen icon, and then select the pen color. That's all there is to it!

You can also use this with Cricut Access – if you're planning on using this a lot, it might be worth it.

To insert the pens into the Cricut machine, you want to choose to make it, and from there, you'll then go to the prepare mat screen. It will say draw instead of writing in the thumbnail this time around, so you press continue in the bottom right-hand corner, then put the pen into clamp A – you just unlock it and then put it in. Wait until it clicks, and that's it!

Cricut pens are super easy, and it's a great idea to consider trying these out.

As you can see, there are many different Cricut features and a lot of functions that may seem complex, but as you can see are really not that hard. There are tons of options for your Cricut projects, and a lot that you can get out of this machine.

Learn How To Edit The Text In Cricut Design Space

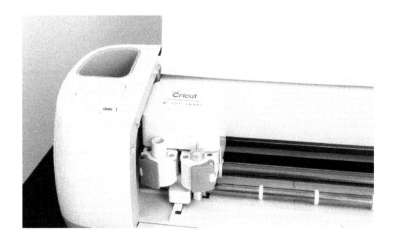

Left Panel Cricut Design Space

Left Panel With the top panel (just explained in detail) you will edit all your designs.

However, where are they all from? All come from Left Panel Cricut Design Space.

This panel is all about inserting forms, pictures, and more. From here, you'll add all the things you're cutting.

This panel has seven options:-New: to produce and replace a new canvas project.

Templates: this enables you to guide the kinds of things you'll cut. Let's say you want to iron on one'sie's vinyl. When selecting the template, you can design and see how it looks.

–Projects: add the Cricut Access project cut ready.

–Images: select single pictures from Cricut Access to generate a project.

–Text: Click to add Text to your canvas region.

–Shapes: Insert all forms on the canvas.

Uploads: upload pictures, cut files to the program.

There's something essential to consider on this panel; unless you've got Cricut Access, Cricut Images, prepared to cut projects, and Cricut fonts cost cash. If you use them, you'll have to pay to cut your project.

Now, we saw a little preview of what this panel was all about. Let's see what happens when you press each button.

New

When you click on NEW, and if you're already working on a project, you'll receive a warning at the top of the window asking if you want to replace your project.

If you want to replace your project, ensure you save all the changes from the current project; otherwise, you'll lose all the hard work. After you save, a new, vacant canvas will open for you to start.

Cricut Design Space Canvas New-1b.

Templates

Templates assist you to see how your project fits on a specific surface. I believe it's just out of this globe.

To customize fashion products, this tool is fantastic because you can choose sizes and distinct kinds of clothing. They also have many different categories to choose from. To know more about templates and how to use them, I suggest reading this article.

Note: templates are for visualization only. When you complete designing and submit your project, nothing will be cut.

Projects

If you want to cut, Projects is where you want to go. You can customize it once you pick your project, or click create it and follow the cutting directions.

Most projects are accessible to Cricut Access members, or you can buy them as you go. However, there are a couple of projects, FREE to cut depending on your device. Just scroll to the bottom of the drop-down menu and pick the device you own.

Canvas Left Panel projects

How to Edit Images In Upload?

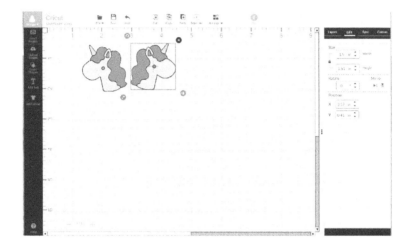

Changes Images in Cricut Design Space Using the Slice Tool

Utilize the Slice device to enable it to change images in Cricut Design Space. Most likely still use that procedure for pictures that is of now transfer to Cricut Design Space.

How to utilize the Slice apparatus to change images.

1. Add your transferred picture to your canvas in Cricut Design Space by tapping on the photo and after that clicking Insert Images. You have the choice of including more than one image at once to your canvas.

2. Make your picture somewhat higher so you can take a shot at it by tapping on the correct base corner and hauling it down a piece. Sufficiently far so you can see it better.

3. In the image I transferred, I need to dispose of the canine. I don't perceive any delete choice on the canvas, so I am going to remove the pooch utilizing the Slice apparatus. Click on Shapes in the left side tool kit; at that point, click on the square.

4. Open the square by tapping on the left base hover beneath the square. Do you see lock symbol? Click on it. Presently you can move the square in any shape you need by utilizing the correct base circle. Then nut the square over the part I was to delete, the pooch.

5. With the square being clicked or featured; on your console press and hold the move caught. With your mouse click the air pocket picture, well, bubble for me. This features them both.

6.With both the square and the image featured, click the Slice apparatus on the base right corner.

7. Start dismantling the bits of your cut endlessly. There ought to be three pieces. You can erase them.

8. Proceed with this procedure until your picture is altered how you need.

Changing Images in Cricut Design Space When Image is uploaded

1. You should transfer a picture from your PC for this procedure to work. When you move it, click complex, and the following window is the place the enchantment occurs.

2. On the upper left corner do you see the wand? Click on it and afterward click on her hair. At that point, snap proceed and name the picture. Snap spare.

It's gone, and it indeed was that simple. Presently, you should deal with her body.

3. You have to transfer the images once more. This time you will be dealing with eradicating the body. First click on the enchantment wand again to eliminate the face, arms, body, and any parts that are more earnestly to get to. When you have that done, snatch the eraser to tidy up the remainder of the body till it is no more.

At the point when the picture is just as you would prefer, click proceed, name your image and afterward snap spare.

Supplement the two images on to your Cricut Design Space canvas when you have them where you can assemble them back.

One reason I am excited about this procedure is that occasionally I need to change things, similar to the hair shading. On the off chance that I left the picture like it was, I couldn't alter the hair shading.

It is important to say that you are as energized as I am to figure out how to *Edit Images* in the Cricut Design Space.

Presently, go forward and create.

ANOTHER STRATEGY

<u>Step by step instructions to transfer and adjust an SVG record in Cricut Design Space</u>

Working with SVG documents in Cricut Design Space isn't in every case, plain and basic. Now and then the SVG you're needing to utilize needs a bit of changes or has a few defects in it. There's quite often an approach to fix or change an SVG record in Cricut Design Space. I've assembled this post with an instructional exercise and video on the most proficient method to transfer and amend an SVG document in Cricut Design Space.

What is an SVG FILE?

For one thing, what is an SVG document? SVG represents Scalable Vector Graphic. They are all the more regularly known as cut documents in the Cricut world since these are the records you transfer into design space that come prepared to cut, well generally at any rate. You don't need to expel any of the foundation or undesirable segments of the design.

How to transfer an SVG FILE

- *First:* to transfer an SVG record buy and spare the material you need to use to your work area or an organizer of your decision. Make a point to name it something you will recall and perceive as SVG records don't demonstrate a thumbnail photograph.

- *Second:* Open Cricut Design Space and select "New Project." When the venture is open head down to the base of the left side device bar and selects "Transfer."

- *Third:* When the transfer screen comes up, select "Transfer Image" at that point, you will either peruse for your picture or intuitive it into Design Space. (The drawing ought to show up in a view box with a blue and white checker foundation. This demonstrates there is nothing behind your picture. Everything indicating blue and white checkers will be clear or void when you start working with your design. This is actually what you need from an SVG.) Next, name your document and hit spare. Your record is then moved into your transfer segment alongside every other material you've transferred.

- *Fourth:* Select the SVG you just transferred into Design Space and hit "Supplement Image." You currently have the SVG in your undertaking, and you can work with it any way you'd like.

How to change an SVG file in Cricut Design Space

In some cases, you're going to need to do some changes. This advanced guide will give you a few hints and deceives here.

Tip one: If you need to do any changes whatsoever to your document the absolute first thing you should do is *UNGROUP* the record. To do this, select the file (feature the material) and head toward the right side menu bar and hit "ungroup" in the top area of the layers board.

Tip two: When the document is ungrouped, you would then be able to utilize the eye symbols to conceal any layer of the design, you do not have any desire to use.

Tip three: You can likewise utilize the shaping instrument at the base of the correct side apparatus bar to expel any little, unattached pieces from your design — more on the most proficient method to utilize the shape apparatus head over to this post.

With the goal that's practically all on the best way to transfer an SVG to Cricut Design Space. Look at the video beneath with more detail on the best way to change an SVG record in Cricut Design Space once you have it transferred.

Utilizing Images in Design Space

The Cricut Image Library contains more than 50,000 images, with all the more being included regularly. You don't have to claim a picture to give it a shot - Cricut Design Space enables you to design with a picture before you purchase so you can ensure it will deal with the venture. Furthermore, you can transfer your very own images and cut them out with your Explore or Maker machine.

Note: Available images may differ by area dependent on picture permitting understandings.

1. Sign in to Design Space and make another task.

2. Click Images on the left half of the design screen for Windows/Mac PC, or tap the Image catch at the base left corner of the screen in the iOS/Android App.

3. Here you can peruse, search, and channel images as required.

- All Images - View included images or quest for a particular picture from the whole Cricut library.

- Categories - Browse for images by choosing one of the picture classes.

- Cartridges - Peruse an in sequential order rundown of more than 400 Cricut cartridges (picture sets) or quest for a particular one.

4. You can choose various images and add them into your task simultaneously.

5. Once the images are embedded, you can adjust them as required for your task. The bounding box is the case that shows up around your content

when it is chosen. Each side of the bounding box enables you to cause a fast to adjust.

- Top left — erase the picture

- Top right — pivot the image

- Bottom left — lock/open the picture extents

- Bottom right — size the picture

Procedure summary

Picture Tile - Preview of the picture.

Data - Click the data catch to see the name of the picture, your degree of access (e.g., possessed, bought in, free, or accessible for procurement), the picture number, the cartridge (picture set) it has a place with (if available). Come back to the picture, see by tapping the data catch once more.

Upgraded Printable Images – Images that are designed with enriching designs and are prepared to print at that point cut.

Cricut Access Content - The picture is included in Cricut Access. This image will show up whether you have a functioning Cricut Access plan.

Maintenance and Troubleshooting

The first and best way to maintain your machine is to keep clean always and ensure that you follow the safety guidelines of the manufacturer. These guidelines always accompany the machine therefore, take your time to read through it. It will save a lot of time and money following these guidelines. But the Cricut Design Space is cloud based so, how can you maintain it? Of course, it is true that it is cloud based but it requires a machine to run it. So, if the machine is sick, how will you work efficiently?

The role of maintenance in any working machine or device cannot be overemphasized because its helps you get higher value for money spent with the increase in efficiency and lifespan of your machine.

What if there are error codes displayed on your Cricut Design space and you are confused on how best to solve them. Do not worry, we will discuss these errors commonly displayed, what they are and how you can solve them here.

Error Code

Every electronic device pops up error when there is a conflict with its program. The Cricut Design Space is no exception because it is also a program running on your device and will also complain if something is missing from its chain of command. As a user interface, it will report this error to you for correction in order to complete its current task.

Let us describe some of these errors and how to troubleshoot them. If you still cannot solve the problem after going through these steps or the error is not treated here, please feel free to contact Member Care. Hey will help you solve it or give the best advice on how to overcome the challenge.

How to Troubleshoot Error codes

There are different error codes which have been discussed below:

Error (0)

1. Restart your computer and machine.
2. If your device is short of that then, ensure that your computer or device satisfy these minimum requirements or try to use another computer or device that meet the requirements.
3. Clear your cache, browser history, cookies and ensure that your browser is updated to the current version.
4. Recreate the project if only one and not multiple project is affected.
5. *Use another computer or device if the above troubleshooting options fail.*

Errors (-3), (-10) *and* (-19)

Note that errors: (-3) refers to "Device Already in Use" error; (-10) refers to "Device Not Open" error; and (-19) refers to "Device Already Open" error. To troubleshoot these errors, follow the following steps.

1. Refresh your machine and then try to cut again.

2. Ensure that the New Machine Setup ran to the end without skipping any step because skipping step(s) can cause these errors.
3. Check the power button display light. If the color is green, then it means you are using a machine that has compatibility problem with Cricut Design space.

a) If the power button is steady/solid red with no other button lit, then try a different power outlet.

b) If the power button is blue, it then means that the Maker is communicating with the Design space through Bluetooth.

c) If the power button is white, then all is well and there is no need to worry. This is the standard color.

d) If the power button is blinking red when you power on the Maker or when update of firmware is in progress, then you need to contact Member care.

e) If the power button is blinking red when you are loading the mat, then do the following:

    i. There may be dust on the roller bars. Turn off your machine and manually move the carriage car over the roller bars for up to 4 times to clear the dust or debris.

    ii. If this did not solve it, contact Member Care.

4. Restart your computer or turn off your device for some seconds and power on again before opening the Design Space to continue your project.

5. Use a different browser for the cut operation.

6. Use a different USB cable.

7. *If not solved after all the steps have been followed, contact Member Care for further assistance.*

Error (-11): "Device Authentication" error

1. Close all background programs on your computer or device and then try again.

2. *Check to see that your browser is updated to the current version.*

Error (-18): "Device Timeout" error

1. Switch off your computer or device

2. Close Design Space

3. restart the Design Space

4. Power on the Cricut maker and then try to cut again.

5. *If no solution, contact Member Care*

Error (-21): "data transmission" error

1. Clear your cache, browser history and cookies

2. Close your browser, re-launch it again and then try cutting

3. Use a different browser to try cut

4. Check your internet speed and ensure that it meets the minimum requirement

5. *Contact your Internet Service Provider (ISP) for assistance*

Error (-24): "Ping Timeout" error

1. Recreate the project because it is possible that the project file is too large or is not properly saved
2. Try another USB port on the computer or make use of Bluetooth
3. Use a different USB cable.
4. Check your internet speed
5. *If nothing works, try a different computer*

Error (-32): Firmware Not Available" error

1. Since this error pops up only when there is compatibility problem, check the connectivity of your device to the Cricut machine.
2. *if you are 100% sure that the connectivity is correct, then contact Member Care for assistance*

Error (-33): "Invalid Material Setting"

1. Check the Smart Set Dial. This error appears when there is no selected material from the Design space and the Smart Set Dial is set to "Custom". Therefore, ensure that a material is selected from the Design space material drop down menu.
2. Try a different material setting.
3. Contact Member Care for assistance.

Inside Looks at Getting the Most Out of Your Cricut

Frequently Asked Questions

This section will feature the questions that are asked most frequently amongst the DIY and crafting community, as well as the community of faithful Cricut users. These questions will span subjects that cover various steps of the crafting process. If there are questions you have, which aren't listed here, check the section later on in this chapter which addresses online resources and popular blogs which address FAQs and common difficulties.

Why can't I weed the design off my backing sheet without it tearing?

The two most common reasons for this issue can easily be remedied. The first reason is a dull blade. Having a dull blade in your Cricut machine can cause snagging or imprecise cuts that can lead to difficulty with pulling the design away from the blank material. There are ways to sharpen your Cricut blades, and Cricut offers very cost-effective blade replacements for purchase on their official website, as well as in retail establishments nationally. The second most common reason for this is the buildup of adhesive or craft material residues on your blade, causing imprecise cuts that can lead to tearing. Remember to stay patient when weeding your designs!

Do I need to convert all my design elements into SVGs?

In short, no. You do not need to convert any of your design files to SVGs in order to use them in Cricut Design Space. If your images are JPG or PNG, they will work just fine in Cricut Design Space. If you would like to convert them, there are several online resources that you can use to help you to do so. Do keep in mind that the SVG file type is slightly more prohibitive in the capabilities that Cricut Design Space has to manipulate them, but they can be better suited to other purposes.

Where is the best place for me to buy materials to use with my Cricut?

Buying materials for your Cricut is one of the least restrictive parts of the whole process. There is nearly an unlimited number of things that you can use with your Cricut to make stunning crafts and, as such, the places in which to get them are similarly unlimited. Crafting and fabric stores will sell ideal materials in droves, and crafting stores are all over the country.

As you continue to gain familiarity with how Cricut works, what you can do with it, what projects are available, you will be more able to find the things that you can use to create dynamic and beautiful projects. As you shop around, you will get better at finding the best materials for the best possible price. In short, just about anywhere!

Is it necessary for me to have a printer to use my Cricut?

It is not required that you have a printer in order to use your Cricut machine. The materials you can buy have colors, patterns, and prints you can choose from in order to give your project the style that you wish for it to have.

In cases when you have found materials that have printable surfaces, you can make use of Cricut's print then cut feature to line up the items you've printed in such a way that they can be cut out and used in your design. Adding the element of a printer to your Cricut crafting is something that can be done (or not done) completely at your discretion.

Is there more than one place for me to get images to use with Cricut Design Space?

This is one of the many beautiful things about crafting with the Cricut system and Cricut Design Space. Any images you can find and save to your computer are images you can import and use in Cricut Design Space. So long as you have the proper licensing to use the image for projects and distribution, and so long as the files are in the proper formats, there aren't any limitations on what you can implement into your design or how you can manipulate them so they fit the vision for your design.

Do all of my fonts have to be purchased through Cricut Design Space?

There are hundreds of fonts available to the average Cricut user and there are hundreds more that you can buy for your designs. However, these are *not* the only fonts you're limited to using. If you can find a website that offers fonts that fit your style better, you can buy or download them, install them on your computer, and then those fonts will be available for you to choose under the "System Fonts" heading in the fonts dropdown menu.

A word of caution, however, if you are looking to use a font for a project, take a look at the licensing information for it. Fonts that are marked "100%

Free" on other websites will generally allow you to use that font on reproductions and things that you sell, while others will require a more involved license fee or subscription.

Why does the Cricut blade keep cutting through the carrier or backing sheet of my material?

This is often due to a project being run through your Cricut on an inappropriate material setting on the dial on the top of your Cricut Explore machine. This dial tells the Cricut how much pressure to exert on the blade, so if you set it for a thicker material than the one you're currently using, you will find that the blade will cut a little bit more deeply than perhaps you would like it to.

Additionally, this could be due to the blade being improperly seated in its housing. Pop open the Cricut accessory clamp, open the housing, and ensure that the blade is not sticking out too far. Once you've checked it, load it back into the Cricut and try again!

My images aren't showing up correctly on the preview screen of my mat; why is this?

It is possible to find that, once you click "Make It," you don't exactly get your design elements laid out quite the way in which you imagined they would be. In some cases, this wonky layout will also mean that those shapes are plotted outside of where your material is on the mat. If you're in this situation, go back to Cricut Design Space, highlight all the images in the design grid, click "Group," then click "Attach." This should bring everything back around to where it should be on the preliminary Make It screen.

Will I need to buy all the Cricut accessories and tools before starting my first project?

No! The tools that you will want to have on hand are:

- **Weeding Tool** – This is a hook with a very fine point that allows you to peel blanks from your cut vinyl. This tool will come in handy for most, if not all the projects you do with your Cricut. It helps you to remove your design from the excess material without having to bend, fold, or fight with your material. This helps to keep the edges of your design crisp, clean and sharp every time.
- **Scraper/Burnishing Tool** – This simple little tool might seem unassuming, but you will find that this tool will be the most commonly used one in your projects, with the exception of

perhaps the weeding tool. You will find that once your designs are lifted from the backing sheet, transferring them to your project surface will require burnishing with even pressure from your scraping tool. Many crafters have found that, in a pinch, this tool can be replaced with other items, but the fine edge, rigid material, and rounded back of this tool are ideal for the job.

– **Scissors** – Any crafter that is worth their salt knows the value of a good pair of scissors. Having a pair of scissors that can make clean and precise cuts is just about the most valuable thing that a crafter can have at their disposal. While the scissors that Cricut offers are exceedingly sharp with fine points and blades, there are other pairs of scissors on the market that will suit your crafting needs and purposes quite well.

– **Craft Tweezers** – The craft tweezers that Cricut offers are reverse-action tweezers that have a strong grip that is exerted at very precise points and can alleviate the cramping that can come from prolonged use. Thanks to the ergonomic grip, it's possible to keep an iron grip on your materials throughout your project so you can keep everything where you need it when you need it there. It's almost like having that extra pair of hands you always wished you had during your crafting projects!

– **Spatula** – Sometimes you might find that you need a little extra control and maneuverability over your project, which might make you call out for an extra pair of hands. This spatula can offer that control and maneuverability that you require, when and where you need it.

You will find that, with the help of the above tools, you will be able to complete your first Cricut project with ease and that you will be able to get a spectacular result every time you work on your crafts.

To find a more comprehensive list of all the supplies you will need before starting your first project, revisit chapter three for the section **What Supplies Will I Need?**

If I buy an image in Cricut Design Space, am I allowed to use it more than once?

Once you buy an image through Cricut Design Space, you are free to use that image as many times you like while you have an active account with Cricut Design Space! Feel free to buy and reuse as many images as you'd like!

I welded two images by accident. Is there an unweld option?

At this time, there is no dedicated unweld function, so you will need to catch this mistake quickly and use the "Undo" command to revert them back to their pre-welded state. You can also delete the design elements and import them in again if you find that you have come too far since welding the images to undo the process. It is recommended that you frequently keep local copies of your work so you can start from various stages if something should go wrong at one stage or another.

Can I turn off the grid in Cricut Design Space, so I have an open space to work with?

Yes, this is something that you can toggle on and off in Cricut Design Space. On a Windows or on a Mac computer, you can open the "Account" menu.

This is marked by the three horizontal lines in the upper left corner. Once you've clicked on that, you will be able to select "Settings." This will present you with numerous settings for your Cricut Design Space and your account. Among them, you will find a section for Canvas Grid settings. This is where you can select your grid preference. In the settings menu, you will also see a section pertaining to Keyboard Shortcuts. Select that in order to set a Keyboard Shortcut that will allow you to quickly toggle the grid on and off while you work on your projects.

When you're working in the Cricut Design Space iOS app, you will find the toggle for the gridlines in the settings at the bottom of the screen. You may have to swipe left to view all the settings that are available to you.

How do I change my Cricut Design Space to operate on the metric system?

This is something that you can toggle on and off in Cricut Design Space. On a Windows or on a Mac computer, you can open the "Account" menu.

This is marked by the three horizontal lines in the upper left corner. Once you've clicked on that, you will be able to select "Settings." This will present you with numerous settings for your Cricut Design Space and your account. Among them, you will find a section for setting the default measurement to inches or centimeters.

If you're using the Cricut Design Space on your mobile device, your settings menu will be at the bottom of your screen. You may need to scroll or swipe to the left in order to see all the options that are available to you.

Do Windows, macOS, and Android have access to the "despeckle" and "smooth" tools?

As of right now, those tools are exclusively available to users who are on the iOS or mobile Apple platform. There are no indications as to whether these tools will be made available to users who are on the Windows, macOS, or Android platforms for Cricut Design Space.

Is it possible for me to upload sewing patterns that I have made to Design Space?

If your sewing patterns are in any of the following formats, you will find that you can upload them to the Cricut Design Space! Accepted formats are: .SVG, .JPG, .BMP, .PNG, .GIF, .DXF.

It should be noted that SVG files will stay their designed size when uploaded into the software, but all vectors are imported as cut lines. Once your image is uploaded, if your pattern contains pattern markings that should be drawn with a fabric pen, you will need to make sure that you change the right lines to write lines, and use the Attach tool so that they will write on your pieces where you need them to write.

What is SnapMat?

SnapMat is an iOS-exclusive feature that gives you a virtual mat preview. This enables you to line up your designs in Design Space, so they'll fit perfectly onto what you have laid on your mat. This feature allows you to place images and text over the snapshot of your mat so you can see exactly how your layout should be in the Design Space.

What Are the Advantages of Using SnapMat?

SnapMat gives you clarity and certainty in where your images will be placed when you send your design to cut through your Cricut. It will show you where your images will be marked, cuts will be done, and how text lines up with other elements. With SnapMat, you can tell your Cricut to cut out a specific piece of a pattern you have stuck on your mat, write in specific areas of gift tags, stationery, cards, or envelopes, and you can get the absolute most out of your materials scraps and spare materials that are left from past projects!

Can I snap multiple mats at one time with SnapMat?

SnapMat can only snap one mat at a time. If you'd like to snap multiple mats, you can do so individually. This ensures that each mat is properly in focus and view and that each one is captured and cut with precision.

Does SnapMat allow me to save the photos of my mats?

SnapMat doesn't currently have a "Save" feature for the images captured in it, so if you would like to retain a photo of your mat, simply take a screenshot in the middle of that process. This will save an image of your mat directly to your photo gallery.

If you find yourself referring to the image for where you have items on your mat, it may be a good idea to wait until you're ready to move on to the next phase of your project.

When it comes to where the cut lines will be on my mat, how exact is the SnapMat feature?

The SnapMat feature is very precise and the lines should be accurate to within a tiny fraction of an inch. While it's best to always give yourself extra space or breathing room when you lay your projects on your mat, you will find that the SnapMat feature is quite exact.

How do I make sure that the mat I have will be compatible with SnapMat?

The SnapMat feature is compatible with all of the Cricut mats that are currently on the market. If you have an older mat or a mat from another company, you might find that you have difficulty. Two of the main things that will cause you difficulty with your mat and this app are black gridlines and bold designs on the mat. These things could confuse the program and could throw off its ability to calculate distances between design elements.

Can I upload images to Cricut Design Space using my Android Device?

Yes, you can! Cricut knows how important it is for their users to be accessible to its users who are on the go. As such, this feature has been made widely available on all existing platforms that support Cricut Design Space, from MacOS to Android.

What sorts of images am I able to upload through Cricut Design Space iOS and Android apps?

Any images that are of supported file types in your photo gallery or saved to your Apple or Android mobile device may be uploaded to Cricut Design Space through your application. If you have SVG, JPG, or PNG files saved to your device, simply upload them and you will find that you're set to go!

If you are attempting to upload a PDF or a TIFF file, you will find that Cricut Design Space does not currently support those file formats. If you're having trouble uploading your images, ensure they're not one of these two formats before trying again!

If my hands aren't quite steady, can I still use SnapMat?

Yes! Many Cricut users have found that balancing their phones on the edge of the table and placing the mat on the floor beneath it is a great way to get a stable shot!

How do I delete any images that I've uploaded through the mobile app?

Another great feature that Cricut decided to make available to suit the needs of all its users is the ability to delete images from Cricut Design Space using any device that supports the application. Whether you're using macOS, Windows, iOS, or Android, you can complete this action on your device.

Simply select the Upload option in the bottom list of options. You may need to swipe or scroll to find this option. Once you've tapped that option, select the Open Uploaded Images option. Once you've navigated to this point, you can find the image you wish to delete. Tap the Info button, which is the little green circle with the lower case I in it. This will give you the option to delete the image and voila! It's gone!

Can I upload images to Cricut Design Space while I'm offline?

Uploading images is an action that can only be completed with an active and stable internet connection. You will find this to be true of uploading to any platform or application that is web-based or cloud-based. Once an image is uploaded with a stable internet connection, however, it can be accessed and downloaded to other devices to offline use.

What Features are Available on Which Apps?

This handy chart will lay out exactly what features are available to you through the Cricut Design Space, as well as the platforms that have enabled support for each feature. Be sure to consult this chart if you're trying to figure out which platform works best for you and the crafting experience that you're looking to have.

Feature	Desktop Computer	iOS App	Android App
3D layer visualization		✔	
Offline		✔	
Photo Canvas		✔	
Smart Guides		✔	✔
SnapMat		✔	
Attach	✔	✔	✔
Bluetooth compatible	✔	✔	✔
Contour	✔	✔	✔
Curve Text	✔		
Cut & write in one step	✔	✔	✔
Flatten to print	✔	✔	✔
Image upload	✔	✔	✔
Knife Blade cutting	✔		
Link Physical Cartridges	✔		
Machine setup	✔	✔	✔
Pattern fills	✔		
Print then cut	✔	✔	
Slice and weld	✔	✔	✔
System fonts	✔	✔	✔
Templates	✔		
Writing style fonts	✔	✔	✔

Cricut Hacks

1. Use a pegboard to store all your Cricut tools, as they all come equipped with that super handy eyelet at the ends of their handles!

2. Ikea offers grocery bag holders that have a circular pattern in them. This pattern happens to make them perfect holders for rolled up Cricut materials that you're not currently using.

3. Use a lint roller to clear debris and dirt from your Cricut cutting mat or from the fabric before you layer it onto your mat. Doing so could extend the life and the grip strength of your mat.

4. Though Cricut strongly advises that you do not clean your Cricut cutting mats, you can use non-alcohol wipes to give them a quick wipe down and to remove any stray detritus.

5. Though Cricut strongly advises that you do not clean your Cricut cutting mats, you can use a gentle soap, cool water, and a gentle scrubber to remove some of the dust and grime that can shorten the life of your cutting mat. **It's imperative not to use hot water or to scrub too hard, as this could ruin the grip on your mat.**

6. Clean your blades by making a small ball of aluminum foil and gently puncturing it with your blades that need to be sharpened. This will also remove any grim that has become stuck on your

blades as well. You can also layer aluminum foil onto your Cricut cutting mat and cut a design out of it. This is a very effective way to sharpen your blades.

7. Leave the material dial on your Cricut Explore set to custom. This way, it will prompt you to select the material type at the beginning of each cutting process. You will never allow your Cricut to cut your materials on the wrong setting again!

8. If you're not into the "Custom" setting idea, you can make a gorgeous self-adhesive vinyl design for the top of your Cricut Explore that will remind you to change your settings at the beginning of every project!

9. If you're getting ready to start a particularly large or intricate project, run a quick test to make sure that your blades are sharp enough, your cuts are coming out right, your blades are seated properly, and everything is in order.

10. If you're burnishing a design onto a canvas that is stretched over a wood frame, you might find that the pressure you put on the canvas only stretches it or doesn't give you the pressure you need. Stick your design thoroughly to the front of your canvas, then flip it onto its face. Using your burnishing tool, scrape in all the places where the design would be on the front. This allows you to exert pressure onto a flat surface without direct contact.

11. When you're removing your transfer tape from a design, it's best to do so by rolling it back off of your design. Pulling directly upward can cause trouble and can cause your design to come up stretch, or bubble in places.

12. If you're having trouble getting your vinyl to lie down properly on the work surface you've chosen, try using some mild heat from something like a hair dryer to get the adhesive to melt just a little bit and grip the surface beneath it.

13. If you're trying to iron a design onto a particularly small or tight place on something, you might try using your hair straightener to apply the heat that it needs to adhere to your surface. Keep an eye on the heat and keep an eye on your design every couple seconds.

14. Teflon sheets are commonly used to diffuse the heat between your iron and your iron-on designs. You might find that parchment paper can make a suitable replacement on certain occasions, though you will want to check on it periodically to ensure that the paper doesn't scorch.

15. If you're trying to line up a vinyl design on the outside of a drinking glass or vase, you can fill it with water, up to the point where you would like to put your design on the glass. Doing it this way will

act as a level for you, so you can be sure your designs aren't crooked!

16. When storing your Cricut marker pens, try storing them upside down. Doing so will help the ink flow to the tip, keeping them fresh and primed for use in each project.

17. You don't have to stick to Cricut pens exclusively. You might find that other pens that are similar sizes can impart different tip styles, colors and more to your projects.

18. If you can't find pens that are the same size as the Cricut proprietary pens, a rubber pen grip can help you to fill the extra space in the clamp to give you a tight grip.

19. If you can't find pens that are the same size as the Cricut proprietary pens, a rubber band or a hair tie can help you to fill the extra space in the clamp to give you a tight grip.

20. You will find that you can get strong-grip transfer tape through any company that makes transfer tape. Transfer tape of this grip strength is often best suited for things like coarse materials or materials with a glitter coating. Reserve your strong stuff for these types of materials.

21. If all you have on hand is transfer tape that's just a little stronger than you need it to be, stick the tape to the leg of your jeans or to a clean piece of fabric just to minimize its grip by a little bit. You can do this a couple of times to get the grip just right.

22. If you are cutting a particularly delicate or intricate design with your Cricut, consider using the washi setting so your blade cuts the material with the appropriate amount of care and finesse.

23. If your mat is losing grip strength thanks to the debris that has been left behind from previous materials used on it, use a strong grip lint roller to pick up those fibers, dust, and other particulates that are diminishing the strength of your mat grip.

24. If you have laid your designs down and found that there are bubbles in them, use the rounded back of the scraper/burnishing tool to gently coax those bubbles out the sides of your designs to flatten them out and neaten them up.

25. If you find that your design has a large number of bubbles in it after you've pulled up the transfer tape, put the transfer tape back down on the design and burnish it down onto the design with your scraper. Really put some elbow grease into it and rub for longer than you think might be necessary and you will find far fewer bubbles at the end of it.

26. Removing your transfer tape at an angle can be a much more effective way to exert control over your tape, your design, and any imperfections that might form while you're pulling the tape away!

27. Iron-on material, thanks to its high adhesive content, is a great material to use on wood surfaces, particularly untreated or unpainted ones. Take care not to scorch the surface of your wood and make use of a heat gun if possible and you will find that your designs will cling quite readily.

28. The Cricut crafting community is fairly divided on whether or not this is the best way to go, but many have found that weeding your design while it's still stuck to your Cricut mat is like having an extra set of hands to hold that project in place for you while you work. Weeding on the mat comes very highly recommended.

29. If you're cutting a design out of cardstock, you can use a lint roller to pull the blanks out of your design and do some preliminary weeding for you.

30. Some crafters have found that, in a pinch, the tines of a fork will help to lift the pieces of their design off the mat in place of something like a weeding tool.

31. If your burnishing tool or scraper has gone on walkabout, try using an old gift card in its place. There are some things it won't do as well, but it will certainly work in a pinch.

32. Instead of using a Teflon sheet to diffuse the heat between your iron and your iron-on material, you can use a regular piece of cotton fabric. This won't be as perfect for the job, but it will certainly hold the place of a Teflon sheet for a few projects while you work on getting the right materials.

33. If your Cricut blades are getting dull on you and you haven't had the chance to sharpen them, or they haven't responded to sharpening, try increasing the blade pressure. This could get you through a project or two while you wait on your replacement blades to come.

34. If you're not sure of how big to make your design in Cricut Design Space so it will fit the material you have, take measurements of your material. Then, make a shape in Cricut Design Space that fits those dimensions. Now you can layer your design over this placeholder image to ensure that it will fit on the material you have.

35. If you've applied one of your vinyl designs to something, but it didn't' quite come out the way you had planned for it to, a heat gun or a hair dryer can help you to remove the design more easily.

36. Transfer tape should not be thrown out after only one use. You should put it back onto the carrier sheet and store it somewhere safe so you can use it again. Most transfer tapes can be used up to seven times before they need to be thrown out.

37. When you're working with a pen or with a tool that has a cap, place the cap in one of two places. Put it on the end of the tool or pen

and snap it into place so it's always right there with the pen or put it in the storage cup on the top of your Cricut machine. This way, it is always in the same place, you will always have access to it, and your tools and pens won't go dry or dull without their protective caps.

Popular Blogs

This is a list of 41 of the most popular blogs that keep Cricut projects on their websites! If you're looking for places with downloads, tutorials, photos, examples for the projects that you can do with your Cricut, simply look through these blogs and find something that fits your style and your skill level!

100 Directions

https://www.100directions.com/creativity/create-with-cricut/

5 Little Monsters

https://www.5littlemonsters.com/p/cricut-crafts.html

Artsy Fartsy Mama

https://www.artsyfartsymama.com/search/label/Cricut

Celebration Shoppe

https://thecelebrationshoppe.com/category/diy-crafts/cricut-crafts/

Clarks Condensed

https://www.clarkscondensed.com/category/diy/cricut/

Coral and Co.

https://www.coralandco.com/blog/category/crafts/everything-made-with-cricut

Country Chic Cottage

https://www.thecountrychiccottage.net/?s=cricut

Crafting in the Rain

https://craftingintherain.com/category/cricut/

Everyday Jenny

http://www.everydayjenny.com/cricut/

Everyday Party Magazine

https://everydaypartymag.com/?s=cricut

Frog Prince Paperie

https://frogprincepaperie.com/?s=cricut

Giggles Galore

https://gigglesgalore.net/?s=cricut

Sew Simple Home

https://www.sewsimplehome.com/p/free-cut-file-projects.html

Happiness is Homemade

https://www.happinessishomemade.net/?s=cricut

Happy Go Lucky

https://www.happygoluckyblog.com/?s=cricut

Hazel and Gold Designs

https://hazelandgolddesigns.com/category/crafts/vinyl/cricut-projects/

Heather Handmade

https://www.heatherhandmade.com/?s=cricut

Hey Let's Make Stuff

https://heyletsmakestuff.com/?s=cricut

Inspiration Made Simple

https://www.inspirationmadesimple.com/category/creative-ideas/cricut-design-

space-star-challenge/

Jennifer Maker

https://jennifermaker.com/

Liz on Call

https://lizoncall.com/?s=cricut

Love the Day

https://love-the-day.com/?s=cricut

Lydi Out Loud

https://lydioutloud.com/?s=cricut

Make Life Lovely

https://www.makelifelovely.com/?s=cricut

Michelle's Party Plan-It

https://michellespartyplanit.com/category/create/cricut/

Paisley Roots

https://www.paisleyroots.com/search?q=cricut&x=0&y=0

Pineapple Paper Co.

https://pineapplepaperco.com/?s=cricut

PMQ For Two

https://www.pmqfortwo.com/category/cricut/

Printable Crush

https://printablecrush.com/category/tutorials/cricut-projects/

Real Girls Realm

http://www.realgirlsrealm.com/search/label/Cricut

See Lindsay

https://seelindsay.com

See Vanessa Craft

http://seevanessacraft.com/?s=cricut

Sew Woodsy

https://sewwoodsy.com/?s=cricut

Stitches Quilting

https://www.stitchesquilting.com/tag/cricut/

Swoodson Says

https://swoodsonsays.com/category/craft-projects/cricut-projects/

Tastefully Frugal

http://tastefullyfrugal.org/category/crafts/cricut

The Crafty Blog Stalker

https://thecraftyblogstalker.com/?s=cricut

The Happy Scraps

https://www.thehappyscraps.com/category/diy-projects/cricut

The Quiet Grove

https://thequietgrove.com/blog/category/diy/cricut/

The Simply Crafted Life

https://www.thesimplycraftedlife.com/category/cricut-projects/

Underground Crafter

https://undergroundcrafter.com/blog/?s=cricut

Online Resources

All these resources are a great place for you to look when trying to find answers about your Cricut machine, project ideas, hacks, quick fixes, troubleshooting, and support from like-minded crafters with the same passion you have!

Makers Gonna Learn YouTube Channel

https://www.youtube.com/channel/UCammHPYWYI4q3WLbx-TP7GA

Sweet Red Poppy YouTube Channel

https://www.youtube.com/channel/UCyJNp6DNzm56XrPppI8r67Q

Lauren Laski YouTube Channel

https://www.youtube.com/channel/UCLQmXfG9McbtLO7k6A2_nvA

Jennifer Maker YouTube Channel

https://www.youtube.com/channel/UCAaLvz5xOyGDQ5Kun16D7zw

The Official Cricut YouTube Channel

https://www.youtube.com/user/OfficialCricut

Kayla's Cricut Creations YouTube Channel

https://www.youtube.com/channel/UCU1cHVibkUOz5RTilJ6QygA

Auntie Tay YouTube Channel

https://www.youtube.com/user/tetetakneea

A Little Craft in Your Day

https://www.alittlecraftinyourday.com/2018/08/03/10-cricut-hacks-you-probably-didnt-know/

Sweet Red Poppy's Website

https://sweetredpoppy.com/cricut-hacks/

The Pinning Mama Website

https://www.thepinningmama.com/hacks-silhouette-cameo-cricut-save-time-money/

The Cricut Official Website

https://home.cricut.com/

The Cricut Official Pinterest Profile

https://www.pinterest.com/Cricut/

Hey, Let's Make Stuff Website

https://heyletsmakestuff.com/cricut-explore/

That's What Che Said Website

https://www.thatswhatchesaid.net/cricut/

CONCLUSION

Thank you for reading all this book!

The next step is to find projects and materials that excite you and dive right in! I would love to see my readers embrace the vast number of crafting opportunities that now lie ahead of them.

There really is no limit to the amazing things you can do with the tools you've purchased for this craft. They're so versatile and, with your creative power added to that versatility, the sky is the limit!

Finally, if you found this book useful in any way, a review on Amazon is always appreciated!

You have already taken a step towards your improvement.

Best wishes!